MEDEA

Euripides
MEDEA

Translated by Alistair Elliot
Introduction by Nicholas Dromgoole

OBERON BOOKS
LONDON

This translation first published in 1993 by Oberon Books Ltd.
(incorporating Absolute Classics)
521 Caledonian Road, London N7 9RH
Tel: 020 7607 3637 / Fax: 020 7607 3629
e-mail: oberon.books@btinternet.com

Reprinted 1997, 2000

A catalogue record for this book is available from the British
Library.

ISBN: 1 870259 36 X

Cover design: Andrzej Klimowski

Typography: Richard Doust

Printed in Great Britain by Antony Rowe Ltd, Reading.

INTRODUCTION

Nicholas Dromgoole

These days the calmly complacent assumptions of superiority on which so much of European culture is based, are very much under attack. The ancient Greeks called non-Greeks "barbarians", and later Europeans inherited the same racist attitudes. Arnold Toynbee, at whose feet I literally sat as an Oxford undergraduate, since his lectures were so popular there were not enough seats to meet the enthusiastic demand, announced in his *Study of History*, "When we classify mankind by colour, the only one of the primary races...which has not made a single creative contribution to any of our 21 civilisations, is the black race." Undergraduates, their assumptions of inherent superiority suitably massaged, then went back to their own colleges, doubtless to listen to the jazz music that was then the latest fashion, without ever considering where jazz came from. On their walls were daringly novel prints by Picasso, with motifs and forms of representation deliberately and determinedly adopted into Cubism by Picasso from African art. Toynbee was writing dangerously racist nonsense, voicing notions that were widely accepted as the "given wisdom" of the times.

We are wiser now. Black academics, particularly Martin Bernal's "Black Athena", have set out vigorously to redress the balance. We now see the ancient Greeks, not as emerging from nowhere to blaze the trail that led to European wisdom and enlightenment, but as just one of a number of cultures around the Mediterranean, deeply influenced by the Egyptian world so firmly established much earlier and far longer in North Africa. Palaeohistorians tells us that intelligent human life originated in Africa's Rift Valley. In that sense, all our origins are firmly African.

Yet it is still important to remember what was special about the ancient Greeks, why we still feel that our culture stems from them, and why we feel that Euripides' play *Medea* still has much to say to us, and why we are entitled to claim a special relationship with ancient Greek drama and regard it fondly and reverently as the founder of our own drama.

Let me first pontificate about that early intelligent human life, even if doing so might make a social anthropologist wince. Since we know so little about early man, my pontificating is as essentially unprovable as anybody else's. Imagine early man in his cave, with thunder and lightning building up a storm outside. These natural phenomena must have been extraordinarily frightening. Yet if they could be explained in terms say, of the anger of the Great God Wuzz, who was angry with us because we had broken his rules, and if early man took his first born to the sacrificial stone at the mouth of the cave and slit his throat to placate the god's anger, what is really happening? The unknowable has become knowable, the uncontrollable has become controllable, and even more importantly, man becomes the centre of the universe since it is all happening because the Great God Wuzz is annoyed with him. It is a truism to point out that much of the force and appeal of early religions depends on this process, making the frightening world explicable, knowable, controllable and reassuring the individual by giving him a false sense of his own importance in the scheme of things. Yet the disadvantages of such religions is that they explain the world in affirmations that demand blind faith and cannot be questioned. If the world is supported, let us say, on the shoulders of a giant, who is standing on a crocodile, supported by a turtle, to question this is blasphemy and such questionings have to be punished.

What was so amazing about the Greeks was that they broke this cultural mould. They seem to have been the first culture known to history prepared to ask awkward questions, and who expected rational answers to such rational questions. In *Medea* Euripides is himself edging his audience towards asking awkward questions about male supremacy. He is appealing to his audience's sense of reason. Belief in the power of reason is a paradox, however, because it is still belief, and there is nothing very rational about belief. Yet

Greek and our culture was built on the belief that there are rational answers to rational questions. The whole of European science is based upon it. Partly, this revolutionary set of expectations, once dazzlingly new, although we now take them for granted, stemmed from their religion which was based firmly on human attitudes, assumptions and wishes. Whatever the range of human desires, from wishing to get drunk, to make love, to work hard, or simply to laze around doing nothing, there was a god or a goddess in the Greek pantheon ready to approve. And feminists will have noted approvingly that there were godesses as well as gods, although Zeus himself, who presided uneasily and very humanly over this squabbling set of deities, was all too male.

The Greeks invented democracy too, even if it was based on slavery, and women were excluded. It is their word. Their system of majority vote, by which the minority agreed to accept the will of the majority, although maintaining the right to argue against the majority and try to convince those who disagreed with them, has remained as a tantalising ideal of how to arrange matters between ourselves ever since.

Neither the ancient Egyptians, nor the Persians (the Greeks' powerful and frightening neighbour), shared that belief in democracy and in that power of reason. Both had autocratic systems and closed theologies. This made the Greeks different and special, so much so that they are correctly regarded as the fount and origin of most of our culture's attitudes and assumptions. J. A. Smith wrote in his *The Unity of Western Civilisation* earlier this century when assumptions of European supremacy were still unchallenged: "We are the Greeks, made what we now are by their thoughts and deeds and experiences, our world their world at a later stage of evolution never interrupted, but always one and single." There is a complacent, Eurocentric air of superiority festooning this statement which we would now more humbly, wish to pare away, but for better or for worse, we cannot get rid of our ties with the Greeks. Like a set of in-laws, they are part of the marriage of our European culture and we are never going to get them out of the house.

Greek theatre has dominated European drama in spite of crucial changes in both the actual buildings and in the conventions of making drama. We are becoming increasingly aware that a mime drama, claiming continuity from ancient Greece, and surviving in fairgrounds and market places, toured Europe until the 18th century. It did not use words and so was able to survive the collapse of the Roman Empire and European disintegration as waves of invasions set up fresh settlements and a bewildering variety of languages. It survived the Dark Ages, flourished in the Middle Ages, and achieved a final flowering in the *Commedia dell Arte* of the 17th and 18th centuries. It cannot be discounted when we are considering Greek influence on our theatre. Scholars have neglected it, largely perhaps because it has no texts for them to argue over.

With classical Greek spoken drama, it has been quite otherwise. This has been an academic battlefield for generations. Partly the trouble has been in the relative paucity of material. Remarkably few plays have survived sufficiently whole for us to make a fair estimate of their quality. It has therefore been relatively easy for academics to become self-appointed experts in Greek drama. They can master the texts, all the available texts, without great effort. Only five Greek dramatists have survived in this way, and one, Menander, belongs to a later century than the rest. The titans were three writers of tragedy, Aeschylus, Sophocles and Euripides, and one writer of comedies, Aristophanes. Of their 44 plays, which have survived, seven are by Aeschylus, seven by Sophocles, and eleven by Aristophanes. The remaining nineteen are by Euripides (484 – 406/7 BC), although one of these is probably by someone else and one is a satyr play written to be performed as an afterpiece to a tragic performance. Even so, we have seventeen plays by Euripides, quite enough to give a fair idea of his powers as a dramatist, although sadly that is a small proportion of the 91 plays we know he wrote.

What of the theatre he was writing for? Here although we know a great deal, every detail is a scholastic minefield.

The large open air auditorium in 5th century Athens, as improved by Pericles, held about seventeen thousand people. It had a raised wooden stage, the *skene,* backed by some sort of scenery and a door for entrances and exits. It was used by actors to play the leading roles. Below it was a large circular space, the *orchestra* or dancing space, used for singing and dancing by the chorus. The *theatron* was the greater part, semicircular rows of stepped seats used by the audience. There were three speaking actors. As they wore masks, they could easily take different parts and did so. *Medea* calls additionally for two children, who appear with their mother on stage. Women's parts were invariably taken by men since women never appeared on the Greek stage. The role of the chorus, (12 to 15 for tragedy, 24 for comedy) was a dramatic convention we no longer share. We think of a chorus as a row of scantily clad and nubile females waving their long legs at the audience. For the Greeks the chorus was an integral part of the drama. At one point they were the centre of attention, dancing and singing lyrics of memorable intensity, which either reinforced or commented on the themes of the play. While the leading actors were on stage, the chorus stood around as respectful spectators of the events on stage, acting as fellow citizens and asking or answering questions, and at a distance, very much part of whatever was going on.

We must remember that drama was still young. Its origins are hidden from us, and can only be a matter of speculation, but we know of no culture that does not possess music, singing and above all dancing, even though some cultures lack what we would call theatre. Singing and dancing can be something everybody takes part in, but gradually can evolve into something done by a specially gifted few, watched and admired by the many. Dance can have an element of narrative, the story of a hunt for example. We can imagine theatre as being born when the story became more important than the dance. In Greek theatre, the song and dance element was still a vital part of the whole, yet already the spoken drama had become differentiated, declaimed by specialist experts from a separate part of the acting area, the stage. The *orchestra*, the dancing space, harked back to an earlier kind of performance.

All Greek spoken drama was part of a religious festival, and the statue of the god of the theatre, Dionysos, was brought from his temple for all to see in the centre of the dancing space, and all the performance was in his honour. We have very little idea of the dance, yet the language of gesture, *cheironomia*, paramount in the mime drama so popular in the market place and in after dinner performances in private houses, still dominated both chorus and actors, and made a common language that must have underpinned the spoken word for the audience, and must have dominated the choreography too.

What we do have is the text, the words the actors spoke. While it is important to emphasise the dance, the singing and the musical elements, Greek theatre was essentially a theatre of the spoken word. Events, dramatic actions, did not take place in front of the audience. All the action took place offstage, and was reported to the characters on stage by a messenger or an eyewitness. This placed great emphasis on the words themselves. Greek dramatists were above all poets. They survived and made their reputations by their ability to say things well. Whatever else may be said about Euripides, he was that rare being, a true poet. His lyric choruses were memorised and recited everywhere. Athenian soldiers made slaves at Syracuse, won their freedom by reciting them. His work set up echoes and associations for his fellow Greeks, that made them well nigh imperishable. Struggling over them in the sixth form at school in the twentieth century, I was still moved by them. It is this quality that makes a translator's task so difficult. We read French and German critics writing about Shakespeare, and it can be like listening to a colour blind man talking about a painting. They are cut off from what is after all the work's greatest glory.

Yet even when translated into an alien language, Euripides still speaks to us across the centuries. It is perhaps pointless to say that he was far ahead of his time, although he was, since that time is so long ago and so much has happened since that he obviously could not even begin to guess at. Regrettably however, human beings still remain obstinately fixed in time as higher primates endowed with instincts and emotions their oversize brains still have difficulty rationalising or understanding. This is Euripides' territory, and to our surprise we discover he can still give us fresh insights into our twentieth century selves, not because so much has altered, but because so little has altered. Relations between men and women are still fraught with difficulties. Male role models still create tensions. Women are still exploited and oppressed.

With remarkably few exceptions, Greek theatre was based on Greek myths, on stories from a fabled past that everybody knew. The audiences always knew how the plot was going to end. Perhaps the best parallel today would be a parish church performance of a nativity play. A modern audience would not sit there wondering what the three wise men would find when the star led them to their destination. The audience knows all that already. The emphasis would be on how the story is treated, how the characters are presented, rather than any suspense about what is going to happen next. All Greek theatre was like that.

Aeschylus belonged to the generation before Euripides. He established with others the basic concept of Greek tragedy as the grandly endowed hero struggling hopelessly against a fate which relentlessly grinds him down. Sophocles, although of Euripides' generation, shared much the same vision as Aeschylus. Euripides was different. While still enmeshed in the same convention that all plays had to be based on myths, he obstinately refused to deal with mythic characters as anything other than ordinary people in unusual circumstances. Even more unusually he is a master of irony. His characters may be saying one thing, but often we know they mean something else. They may be deceiving themselves but Euripides makes sure they do not deceive us. He teaches us to suspect their motives and discount their claims. And even though the plot is already known, he is full of dramatic suprises.

The Greeks were nothing if not competitive, and although it was a six day religious festival, the Great or City Dionysia held each March for which Aeschylus, Sophocles and Euripides wrote among a host of other dramatists, was very much a competition. Three writers of tragedies would each present four plays, making twelve plays in all. The other eleven plays have not survived from the occasion when *Medea* was first presented, but we know *Medea* was placed last in the popular vote. Throughout his entire career, Euripides won only four "Firsts" for his plays, and that represents a mere four out of ninety one plays. Even with the seventeen plays we have, it is clear that audiences must have found him unsettling, a dramatist who was "caviare to the general". He was questioning, even making fun of what his audience took for granted, and few audiences enjoy too much of that.

In the British television series "Till Death us do Part", Warren Mitchell voiced outrageously prejudiced statements about Jews, Blacks, the monarchy and British snobbery, with the clear intention that the audience would respond to all this as satire. Apparently some sections of the television audience reacted in quite the wrong way, lapping up the preposterous prejudices because they shared them, relishing Mitchell's ludicrous views because they coincided with their own. I suspect that sections of Euripides' Greek audience of seventeen thousand must have behaved in much the same way, responding to the excitement of the drama, and the beauty of the language, but missing the irony entirely and positively sharing some of the outrageous views solemnly enunciated by the less attractive characters. Jason's views on women and wives for example. How many Greek males nodded approvingly, blissfully unaware what an insensitive prig Euripides sets out before us. Perhaps by the end of the play they began to feel uncomfortably that they had missed something, and firmly voted against. Every time a man in a

Euripides play speaks about women, irony hangs on his words. Every time women speak about other women, automatically accepting the values of a male dominated society, irony mocks.

Earlier this century, feminists claimed Euripides as one of their own. A careful reading of his plays would not seem to support this. He is very concerned with the relationships between men and women. In a male dominated society he is constantly asking audiences to question men's claims about their attitudes to women, to see how men deceive themselves in their attitudes and assumptions about women, and to recognise what is really going on. In fifth century Athens, as in twentieth England, that in itself is probably revolutionary enough.

At one level *Medea* is a play about a woman's revenge on the man who deserts her. She kills his new wife and she kills the two children she herself has borne him in order to hurt him. Revenge was a more acceptable concept in pre-Christian Greece. Since a hero was bound to defend his own concept of his own honour, one of the ways that was publicly done was by revenging afronts and injuries. A Greek audience would understand about revenge. Killing children was something the Greeks took in their stride too. It was usual to do away with sickly infants, or sometimes infant girls were killed simply because they were unwanted. But the crucial decision of life or death was left to the father. Mothers were thought of as being too emotionally attached to their offspring to be rational about it. So even a Greek audience would have been shocked at Medea's decision to destroy her own children.

The myth was well known. Jason and his Argonauts sailed to Aeëtes' kingdom to win the Golden Fleece. Aeëtes imposed impossible conditions, but his daughter, Medea, fell in love with Jason and helped him meet the conditions. When Aeëtes refused to keep his word Medea helped Jason vanquish the dragon who guarded the Golden Fleece and they both fled the country with the fleece, pursued by Aeëtes. To discourage her father, Medea scattered the route with dismembered bits of her own brother. When she and Jason arrived in Colchis, Medea persuaded the daughters of the ruler, Pelias, that she could rejuvenate Pelias provided they first cut him up in pieces and cooked him. She then refused to do anything and left him well and truly cooked. Jason and she withdrew to Corinth, lived happily and had two children. Then Jason fell in love with King Creon's daughter and abandoned Medea. Medea sent a fine new robe as a present to the new bride, and the robe consumed her with fire as soon as she put it on. Medea then cut the throats of her two children fathered by Jason and fled to sanctuary in Athens where she married King Aegeus.

Euripides uses the myth to expose the complacent cruelty of Jason in his treatment of Medea. It has to be accepted that modern audiences are far more likely to be sympathetic to Medea and appalled by Jason's treatment of her than any Greek audience would have been. Greeks took male superiority for granted. So when Euripides shows us Jason as a conceited prig, unable to grasp Medea's suffering, much less respond to it, he has had to apply a little built in bias against Jason, largely because a Greek audience would otherwise have sympathised all too quickly with the husband.

Medea is far brighter than anyone else on stage. The scenes where she persuades the two older men, Creon and Aegeus, to do what she wants, not what they want, are minor masterpieces of satirical humour. Yet with her husband at first Medea's cleverness fails. She is too wounded, too upset, too emotional. Then she plans her revenge. She wins the acquiescence of the Chorus to the idea of killing the new wife, but then the Chorus find themselves consenting by their silence to the murder of the children. This is a fine dramatic surprise. The audience also, who have been acquiescing all too easily in the murder of the wife, now find themselves facing up to the moral question of the rights and wrongs of killing the children. We can notice in passing how unimportant wives are compared with husbands. Medea wishes to hurt her husband. Nobody sees anything wrong in killing a new wife in order to hurt the husband. The views and fate of the new wife are hardly considered. The theme of the play is clear. How can a mother murder her own children? Is she justified in doing so? The audience observing the appalling insensitivity of the men around Medea, if not condoning her actions, at least understands them and sympathises with her.

Why do men, stripped naked in a modern prison regime, smear their own excrement around the walls? It is a last affirmation of their own individuality, a refusal to accept the humiliations the system is imposing upon them. They use the only weapons available to them. Medea, in determining to show Jason the enormity of his behaviour to her, commits the seemingly inexplicable, but she too is using the only weapons available to her. She has her final triumph and revenge. Yet the final irony is that it has been a hollow revenge. She may have destroyed her husband's happiness, but she has destroyed her own as a mother. Her victory is pyrrhic, long before that battle added a new word to our language. That is the tragedy of any fight between a husband and a wife. Neither triumphs. Both lose. And that implies a dependence between them that few ancient Greek males would have been willing to admit or accept.

London, 1993

TRANSLATOR'S NOTE

This text is more or less the words of Euripides' play as performed in September and October 1992 at the Almeida Theatre, Islington, under the direction of Jonathan Kent. It owes much to his literary understanding and incisiveness.

Every production of a classic play inevitably has its own aims: in our case, we thought we were trying for an uncluttered, transparent, close translation. However, our Choruses are probably clearer and less ambiguous than in the original, while Euripides' lean dialogue has been honed down to a film editor's rapidity. Some of the cuts have been restored here in square brackets [like this]; other passages, like the references to touching beards and knees in the procedure of supplication, have been simply suppressed. It is hoped that the resulting script will be more useful to other producers. We dealt particularly fiercely with the self-conscious ancient game of line-by-line dialogue (*stichomythia*) between Medea and Aegeus, and with the Chorus's important but leisurely discourse on having children; fuller and more literal versions of both these parts of the play (and of the last lines) are offered in an appendix.

I very much regret not being able to give here any idea of Jonathan Dove's haunting and expressive music for the Choral songs, or Peter J. Davison's resoundingly hollow House of Jason (the set), or Jon Morrell's timeless but recognisably Aegean costumes. It is in the nature of theatrical work that it disappears, but I am grateful that I was able to see so many times the wonderful performances of the Almeida cast; Euripides only saw his play once.

MEDEA

Characters

MEDEA
WOMEN OF CORINTH
NURSE
TUTOR
CHILDREN
CREON
JASON
AEGEUS
MESSENGER

This translation of *Medea* was first produced at the Almeida Theatre, London on 10 September, 1992, directed by Jonathan Kent with the following cast:

MEDEA	Diana Rigg
WOMEN OF	Jane Lowe
CORINTH	Nuala Willis
	Elizabeth Bell
NURSE	Madge Ryan
TUTOR	Dennis Clinton
CHILDREN	Stephen Mullin/John Rafferty
	Rowen Hawkins/Oliver Pearce-Owen
CREON	Joseph O'Conor
JASON	Tim Woodward
AEGEUS	Peter Sproule
MESSENGER	Dan Mullane
Set	Peter J. Davison
Costume	Jon Morrell
Music	Jonathan Dove
Lighting	Alan Burrett

Following a UK tour, the production transferred to Wyndham's Theatre, London, on 13 October, 1993, directed by Jonathan Kent with the following changes:

WOMEN OF	Jane Lowe
CORINTH	Nuala Willis
	Stella McCusker
TUTOR	John Southworth
CHILDREN	Blair Dickinson/Ryan Dickinson
CREON	John Turner
AEGEUS	Robert Demeger
Costume	Paul Brown
Music Associate	Matthew Scott

The production then went to Broadway and opened at the
Longacre Theatre, New York, on 7 April, 1994, with the
following changes:

WOMEN OF	Judith Paris
CORINTH	Jane Lowe
	Nuala Willis
NURSE	Janet Henfrey
AEGEUS	Donald Douglas
CHILDREN	Tyler Noyes/Lucas Wiesendanger

A palace near Corinth

Enter NURSE.

NURSE: I wish the Argo had never spread its wings
    And flown to Colchis through the Clashing Rocks.
    I wish the pine tree on the slopes of Pelion
    Had not been felled; not split to feathery oars
    To fledge the arms of Argonauts. Oh why
    Did Pelias send them for the Golden Fleece?
    If they had never come, my mistress Medea
    Would not have sailed back to Iolcos with them,
    Dazed with passion for their leader, Jason.
    Then she would not have made King Pelias' daughters
    Kill their own father. And she'd not have come
    To settle here in Corinth, but she has.

    Here all went well at first: a blameless life
    With husband and with children. Though an alien,
    She did good service to the citizens
    Of her new country, and she fitted in
    As well with Jason's every wish. For women,
    That's the best way to make yourself secure:
    Never stand up and argue with a man.

    But now the house is full of hate; and my dear girl
    Is ill with it. For Jason has become
    A traitor to his children and my mistress.
    He abandons her, to lie in a royal bed:
    He's marrying the king's daughter, Creon's child.
    My poor Medea loses all her rights
    And honours, everything. "He swore an oath,"
    She cries, "He gave his word! I trusted him!"
    She begs the gods to witness this reward
    From Jason, after all she did for him.
    She lies not eating, slumping into grief,
    Melting the hours of life away in tears.
    She never moves her head or lifts her eyes
    From staring at the ground, deaf as a stone

Or wave of the sea to our advice and comfort –
Except, she sometimes turns that white white neck
To look away and mutter to herself
Mourning the father she betrayed, the home
And family she abandoned to come here
With a man who treats her now with such dishonour.
Poor thing, she's learnt at the ungentle hands
Of fortune, what it means to lose your country.
She hates to have her children near; she sees them
And does not smile. I fear she's plotting something,
And she is a woman to fear: if you arouse
The hatred of Medea, don't expect
An easy victory, and to go home singing.
    Here are the children, though. They're fresh from play,
Not thinking of their mother's misery
At all. The young mind runs away from pain.

*Enter MEDEA's two small BOYS, followed by the TUTOR
(child-minder).*

TUTOR: [Old slave, old heirloom from my mistress' home,]
    What are you doing, standing here alone
    Outside, and groaning to yourself? Medea
    Usually wants you with her. Why not now?

NURSE: [Old slave yourself! Servant of Jason's children!]
    A good slave, when the mistress' luck runs out,
    Feels the disaster falling on himself.
    I felt such sympathy with what she suffered
    I had to come out here and tell her troubles
    To the witnesses of earth and air.

TUTOR: So our sad lady has no rest from weeping?

NURSE: I wish I thought so. Her pain has hardly started.

TUTOR: Poor fool – if one may say such things of masters –
    She doesn't know the latest news is worse.

NURSE: What do you mean? Don't keep this to yourself.

TUTOR: It's nothing – I regret I mentioned it.

NURSE: Old man, don't hide it from your fellow-slave.
    I can be silent if I have to be.

TUTOR: I heard, when I was seeming not to listen,
    But standing where the old men sit and play
    At board games, by the sacred spring Pirene,
    Somebody say the children are to be banished
    From Corinth, with their mother. It appears
    That is the king's intention. I don't know
    If this is true – I pray it turns out false.

NURSE: Jason won't let them treat his sons like that.
    He's quarrelling with their mother, not with them.

TUTOR: When new alliances are made, the old ones
    Are dropped behind. His love has left this house.

NURSE: We're sinking from the first of fortune's waves;
    We cannot take another; we shall drown.

TUTOR: Anyway, this is not a time to tell the mistress
    What I have heard: for now, stay calm, and silent.

NURSE: Children, you hear what sort of father you have?
    I curse him – no, I must not – he's my master.
    But we have found him out: he's a bad friend
    To his own family, those he ought to love.

TUTOR: What man on earth is different? Don't you know
    Everyone loves himself more than his neighbour?
    You're slow to learn, but now you see a father
    Can shed affection with a change of bed.

NURSE: Go in – all will be well – boys, go in.

    To TUTOR.

    Keep them as isolated as you can.
    Don't let them near their mother: she's distraught.
    Already, I've seen her eyeing them, like a beast

About to charge. I'm sure she'll never let
Her anger rest until she's struck at someone –
So long as it's her enemies, not her friends.

*Before the CHILDREN and TUTOR can go off, MEDEA
is heard offstage*

MEDEA: (*Scream!*)
    The pain of misery! A world of trouble
    Is falling on me! I want to die!

NURSE: I told you, children: that's your mother
    Raking the anger through her heart.
    Go in quickly, get inside –
    Don't go anywhere she can see you,
    Don't go up to her – just look out
    For her savage mood: she was always wilful
        But now she's wild with hate.
    Go now, run inside; be quick.

The CHILDREN and TUTOR go into the palace.

Clearly now the storm is rising;
The cloud of pain will soon burst
Into greater fury. What will her proud
Untameable spirit do
    Under the bite of suffering?

MEDEA: (*Scream.*)
    I have endured so much! I've earned
    The right to scream. O cursed children
    Of an unloved mother, may you die!
    Die with your father! May the whole
        Family of Jason perish!

NURSE: You poor unhappy woman.
    But why do you make your sons share
    Their father's offence? Oh, why hate them?
    Poor children, I'm sick with fear for you.
    I know something is going to happen.

(*She explains to the children.*)
Strange and terrible
    Are the minds of royal masters:
Always commanding, never obeying,
They have strong moods and cannot change them.
Ordinary life where everyone's equal
Is better, much better. I hope to grow old
In a safe low place, not high and grand.
For man should live with limit and measure;
That is a phrase we often use,
And it's proved true: Going beyond,
Going too far, brings no advantage.
It only means, when the gods are angry,
    They extract a greater price.

Enter the CHORUS, who are Corinthian women.

CHORUS: I could hear the voice, I could hear the cries
    From this unhappy woman of Colchis.
    Is she still no calmer? Tell us, old woman.
    Through the double doors of her inner room
    I could hear the lament – and I take no pleasure
    In the sounds of sorrow that flow from this house:
    The years have made us feel we are friends.

NURSE: The house? The family? That is finished.
    For he is held in a royal bed,
    While she broods in her old rooms,
    My mistress, wasting her hours away
    With not one loving friend beside her
    To warm and comfort her mind with words.

MEDEA: (*Scream.*)
    O fire from heaven, pierce through my head!
    What use is living, now, to me?
    Let me release myself in death
        And leave this life I hate.

CHORUS: Gods of earth and light and sky,
    Do you hear this painful cry,

The song of the unhappy wife?
Crazy wish, to lay your head
In death's abominable bed.
   Oh never rush to finish life
     Oh never pray for that.
And if your husband turns from you
And starts to worship someone new,
Don't scratch your cheeks and pull your hair
     Because he's leaving.
     I know it hurts,
But Zeus will see that you get even;
Jason will get his just deserts.
So don't lose heart because you lose a man.

MEDEA: Oh father, my city! My lost home!
   What I left behind when I killed my brother,
   When I killed my own brother, to get away!
   Great goddess of Justice, look down and see
   What I have to endure from my cursed husband,
   And after I'd bound him with oaths of power!
   How I'd love to tear the palace down
   About the pair of them, crush and grind
   Their bodies together in bloody rubble!
   They started this – they dared to harm me.

NURSE: You hear what she wants? She calls on the gods.
   This is an anger worthy of heaven
     And nothing small will calm it.

CHORUS: How can we make her come out here
   To see us face to face and hear
     The solemn words of good advice?
   We might be able to assuage
   The hunger of her heavy rage.
     I'll always be the sort who tries
       To be of use like that.
   But you go fetch her out of there,
   Out of the gloom into the air.
   Tell her it's friends. We want to help.

Be quick, before
She does some wrong
To someone innocent inside,
Before her passion gets too strong.
I feel the violence gathering in the air.

NURSE: I'll try again.
But I doubt if my mistress will listen to me.
Like a savage beast with new-born young,
She lours, she turns on any servant
Who moves towards her trying to speak.
If only we could charm her with music.
I sometimes think those clever men
Of the past were fools: it was stupid of them
To invent music only for festivals,
Great banquets, and friendly dinners.
They made melodious news of life:
But no one made up a medicinal music,
A treatment of voices and instruments
That would ease the terrible pain of living –
The pangs of death and the downfall of families.
Couldn't they see there'd be profit in curing
Pain with song? [But there at dinner,
At a lovely feast, why do they raise
Their voices and sing? The pleasure of food,
The present meal, is by itself
    Filling enough for mortals.]

Exit NURSE into palace.

CHORUS: I hear the cry of discontent,
    The still-continuing wail.
    I hear the liquid voice lament
    The evil husband, the betrayal.

    Unjustly injured and abused,
    She calls on Themis, that goddess
    Who stands at the right hand of Zeus
    And guards our promises:

It was a promise and an oath
That brought her with the Golden Fleece
Away from Colchis in the night
Across the sea to Greece,

[Through where the lock
And clashing key
Of salty Hellespont still block
The impenetrable Euxine Sea.]

Enter MEDEA.

MEDEA: Women of Corinth, I have come out to see you
For fear you might reproach me. You mustn't think
I'm proud. I know some people hide themselves
From common sight, like gods, and that shows pride,
While others show it stalking down the street.
But some, who just walk quietly, get a name
For being haughty, distant and superior.
The eyes of men are not the fairest judges:
Sometimes, before they know a person's heart,
They hate on sight – when no-one gave them cause.
Foreigners specially have to court a city –
But citizens should try to fit in too.
I think it can't be right for anyone
To stand aloof and simply please themselves –
They offend their fellow-men; it's ignorant, it's wrong.

It's so with me: this unforeseen disaster
Has stunned my spirit. I am lost. The joy
Of life has gone. I even want to die.
You see, someone I should have known so well,
My husband, has turned out the worst of men.

Of all the creatures that have life and reason,
We women are the most unhappy kind:
First we must throw our money to the wind
To buy a husband; and what's worse, we have to
Accept him as the master of our body.

Then comes the question that decides our lives:
Is the master good or bad? It's possible
To change your spouse, but indecent for a woman;
And we can not refuse the man we're given.
We come to new conventions and new ways,
Innocent from home. You'd need to be clairvoyant
To please this stranger who is in your bed.
Suppose we manage all such duties well
And he can live in harness without fretting,
Then life's ideal; but if not, best die.
A man who's tired of what he gets at home
Goes out – and gives his heart a holiday.
But we are forced to look at one face always.
They tell us, "In this life you live at home
You run no risks, while we take arms and fight."
Not true, I say: I'd rather stand three times
In battle by my shield than once give birth.
Of course, the story's not so bad for you:
You have your city here, a father's house,
Pleasures in reach, and company of friends,
But I'm alone, a citizen of Nowhere,
Insulted by my husband, just a woman
He took as plunder from her barbarous country.
I have no mother, brother, any kin
To be my harbour in the storm of fortune.
Therefore I beg this single favour from you:
If I discover some device, some means
To make my husband pay for what I've suffered,
You will say nothing. A woman may be timid
In other ways, too weak to stand and fight
And almost fainting at the sight of weapons,
But when she finds her bed has been defiled,
No other creature has such deadly thoughts.

CHORUS: I promise. It's only fair to make him pay,
    Medea. I don't wonder at your pain.
    (*The other CHORUS members also say: "Promise."*)

But look, there's Creon. The king! He's here
Perhaps to announce some new decree.

Enter CREON.

CREON: You sour-faced woman, squalling at your husband,
Medea, I give you notice: you are banished.
You must leave now. Now! Take your children with you.
Don't make me wait. I shall not leave
Until I've seen you off Corinthian land.

MEDEA: (*A cry.*)
This is the end of everything, my last moment.
My enemies speed me on with all sail set
Toward the rocks – and there's no place to land.
I have been much abused, but I still ask you,
Creon, why are you sending me away?

CREON: I am afraid of you: no need to wrap
The fact in phrases: I'm afraid that you
Might do my daughter some irreparable harm.
And many things contribute to this fear:
You are clever; you have seen and known much evil;
You are wounded, and deprived of bed and man.
And now I hear that you've been making threats
Against me, for giving my daughter to your husband.
I hear you will do something. I must guard against it.
Better to draw your hatred now than soften
And later have to weep for being soft.

MEDEA: (*Laughs bitterly.*)
Oh Creon, this is not the first time: often before
My reputation has done me harm, much harm.
My father, if he'd been wise, would never have had me
Taught to be clever, out of the ordinary.
That only makes you envied and disliked.
Try teaching new ideas to stupid people –
They think you're stupid, certainly not clever;
As for the others, who aspire to wit,

You offend them, too, if you are reckoned wittier.
I've had my share of that experience.
I am clever, so the jealous hate me – or
They find me difficult; but I'm not that clever.
Still, you're afraid of me. What do you think
I'll do to you to spoil your harmony?
You need not be on edge, Creon: look, I'm hardly
In a state for crimes against the crown.
What harm have *you* done *me*? It's my husband I hate,
Not you. You gave your daughter as your heart
                                                     commanded.
That is your right, and seems to me quite sensible.
I don't resent things going well for you:
Celebrate marriage; prosper – all of you.
But let me stay. In spite of being wronged,
I'll keep the peace. You're stronger, and I've lost.

CREON: You seem to answer softly. But I shudder
    To think what evil may be in your mind.
    The softness makes me trust you even less.
    For a hot-tempered woman – or man – is easier
    To guard against than someone quiet and clever.
    So you must leave. With no delay. No speeches.
    The order's fixed. I know you are my enemy,
    And you shall not contrive to stay among us.

MEDEA: I beg you, in the name of your newly-married
                                                     daughter.

CREON: Your words are wasted: you shall not persuade me.

MEDEA: You'll banish me? There's nothing I can say?

CREON: Why should I care for you more than my flesh
                                                     and blood?

[MEDEA: My country! How much I think of home today!

CREON: It's what I care for most – except my children.]

MEDEA: O Love, how great a curse you are to mortals!

CREON: Well, that depends upon the circumstance...

MEDEA: Zeus knows who caused all this: don't let him get
off free.

CREON: Move, woman. Must I have you dragged away?

MEDEA: No, Creon, no – not that. I'm pleading now...

CREON: So are you going to give me trouble? Yes or no?

MEDEA: We'll go, we'll leave – that isn't what I'm asking.

CREON: Why argue then? Why not just quietly go?

MEDEA: One day. Let me stay on for just one day.
Let me think out clearly where it is we'll go,
Make provision for the children, since their father
Puts rather low his duty to his sons.
Take pity on them: you're a father too;
It stands to reason you have kindness in you.
For my part, exile doesn't worry me –
I weep for them: they are so young to suffer.

CREON: I've never had the temper of a tyrant.
Often, from honouring other people's wishes,
I've spoiled things for myself – and even now
I see I might be making a mistake.
Still, you shall have your way. But in advance
I warn you, if the eye of heaven tomorrow
Should see you and your children on my soil,
You die. That is my word. As true as prophecy.
Remain then, if you must, this one day more:
Too short a time for you to do us harm.

Exit CREON.

CHORUS: Poor suffering woman!
Poor, poor wretch, in a world of troubles
Where will you turn? What host, what refuge,
What house or country can you find
That's safe and welcoming? What a sea of pain

The god has set you to sail across,
    Medea, a trackless sea.

MEDEA: (*To CHORUS.*)
    Everything's set in every way against me.
    But don't imagine this is all – not yet.
    There are still dangers for this bride and groom:
    And more than a little *trouble* for her father.
    Do you think that I'd have crawled and fawned on him
    Without some hope of gain, some scheme in mind?
    I'd not have spoken to him, not have touched him.
    But he has reached the depths of folly now:
    He could have banished me at once, and stopped
    My plans – instead, he's given me this day:
    I've time to turn three enemies to corpses –
    The father and the daughter, and *my* husband.

    There are so many paths to death for them –
    I can't decide which route is best to take.
    Shall I light up the bridal house with fire?
    Take a sharp sword and drive it through their hearts?
    I'd slip in silently and find their bed –
    But there's the difficulty: if I'm caught
    On the way in, still working out the plan,
    I'm dead – instead of killing them, I make them laugh.
    The best road is the most direct, the way
    I have most skill: I'll take them with my poisons.
    So be it.
    Suppose they're dead: what city will receive me?
    What host will offer me protection,
    Asylum and a home that's safe? Not one,
    At present. So I'll wait a little yet:
    Either a place of refuge will appear,
    And I can take them by deceit and stealth;
    Or, if the inevitable hour of exile
    Comes first to drive me out, I'll use the sword,
    Though it may cost my life, and go to kill them
    Along the path of bravery and strength.

I swear by all the gods, whom I adore
And whom I call to help me once again,
They shall not laugh at this tormented heart.
I'll make their marriage sour – and painful – to them,
Sour the alliance of their families,
And sour the day they chose to banish me.
Come then, Medea; use every means you know;
Move toward horror: this is the test of spirit.
Remember what they're doing. Don't accept
Their mockery, this marriage of a Jason
To a girl whose ancestor was Sisyphus!
A man who pushes stones uphill in Hades!
They laugh at me, grand-daughter of the Sun!
But I have knowledge to oppose them with:
And also, I'm a woman; so, although disbarred
By nature from the noble deeds of man,
I have mastered all the arts of cowardice.

CHORUS: The water in rivers is flowing uphill.
              From now, upstream means down.
        The laws of nature, the laws of man
                  Are all turned round:
        It's men do the wiles and smiles, the cheating, now,
            It's men will not keep the vows they swore,
        While women now find history reversing
        The low esteem in which they lived before.
        A woman soon will have both rights and honour;
        She won't have gossip holding her in check
                  And spitting insults on her.

        Time-honoured lyrics we used to sing
                  Will have to be rewritten.
        They can't keep saying, "Don't trust a woman,
                  You might get bitten."
        The trouble was, Apollo, god of song,
            Never passed on his poetic fire
        To one of us. He liked us dumb and dancing,
        And chose no woman poet to inspire.

Otherwise, what an ode I'd sing on men!
The ages can tell tales of us, but husbands
　　　Have been as bad again!

Poor woman, you left the king your father's house,
Insane with passion, and on Argo's bows
Parted the double rocks of Hellespont.
　　You came to live in a foreign land,
　　You lost the husband from your bed
　　　And now you lose the bed,
And even that last right, the right to stay:
　　The king is sending you away.

Now words of honour blow away like clouds.
No shame is felt, for Shame has learned to fly –
Shame has left Greece and taken to the sky.
　　You have no home or parent near,
　　Poor wretch, to be an anchorage
　　　Out of this stormy age,
And now a new king's daughter has taken over
　　Your lover's household and your lover.

Enter JASON.

JASON: O this is not the first time; I have seen it
　　Often before: a savage, bristling nature
　　Can do such harm, impossible to deal with.
　　You had, and could have kept, this land and house
　　As home, for the small price of giving in
　　Gracefully to the plans of your superiors;
　　Instead, you froth some nonsense and get banished.
　　To me it doesn't matter: keep on saying
　　How wicked Jason is: "the worst of men";
　　But what you said against the royal house –
　　Count yourself lucky to escape with exile.
　　How often, after you'd enraged our rulers,
　　I had to placate them, wanting you to stay here.
　　But you could not give up your folly, and still
　　You curse the king. So naturally, you're banished.

But even so I won't disown my family –
I come here, woman, still thinking of your future,
So you shan't leave for exile with the children
In need or unprovided: banishment
Brings many hardships. And – though I know you hate me –
I can't imagine ever hating you.

MEDEA: Spineless man! – the only weapon I have
Is words, to attack your failure as a husband!
You come to us, where you're most hated, here?
Is this your courage and heroic boldness,
To wrong your friends, then look them in the face?
No: it's that worst disease of human minds,
A blank where shame should be. But I am glad you came:
It makes my heart a little easier
To spear you with my words, and watch you writhe.

I'll begin at the beginning.
I saved your life, as every Greek can witness
Who joined you in the voyage of the Argo;
[I helped you catch the fire-breathing oxen
And harness them, and sow the fatal field;]
I killed the dragon, the sleepless sentinel
That wound its coils around the Golden Fleece;
I held the light of safety over you.
I chose to desert my father and my home
To come with you to Iolcos: full of love,
Empty of thought, in those days. After that, I killed
King Pelias, using his own daughters' hands
For the unkindest death, to wipe his blood-line out.
I did all that for you, and now you drop me;
You take a new wife, seeming to forget
That we have children. If you were a childless man,
One might forgive your lusting for her bed...
But all your oaths and promises are broken:
I cannot trust you now. Nor can I understand
What you believe in – do you think the gods
That used to govern us no longer do?

You seem to imagine the moral law has changed –
But even you must realise you've not kept your word.
Look at this hand you took in yours so often,
These knees you clung to, begging me to help:
The meaningless embraces of a bad
Husband! The hopes I entertained and lost!

Come on! I shall confide in you, like some old friend –
There's nothing I can gain from you, I know that,
But still – I can expose your shame with questions:
Where can I turn to, now? Home to my father?
I betrayed my home and country to come with you.
To the grieving daughters of King Pelias?
A fine welcome they'd give me
                    In the house where I killed their father.
It comes to this: the friends I had at home
Now hate me; and in other places too
Where I need not have harmed a soul, I did,
Because you asked me to. They hate me now as well.
So in return for that, you made me "happy" –
Greek women think so, anyway: "What a wonderful
And faithful man that lucky woman has!"
This husband who calmly lets me go, to exile,
Without a friend, alone with fatherless children –
A fine beginning for a newly-married man,
That his children and the woman who saved his life
Must wander abroad in cringing beggary.

Oh Zeus, why did you give humanity
The clearest evidence when gold is false –
But set no markings on the skin of man
To single out the bad one from the good?

CHORUS: This is a terrible passion: there's no cure,
    When those who met to love now join to fight.

JASON: So now the bad man must be good at speaking,
    And like the skilful captain of a boat

Brail up the canvas and with shortened sail
Run out from under your noisy squall of words.

You greatly exaggerate your kind assistance.
You claim you saved the Argo expedition.
I have to say I credit Aphrodite
And only Aphrodite, no-one else.
You have quick wits, so it's not necessary –
Indeed it would be indelicate and ungrateful
To list the many ways in which Desire,
Drove you, helpless, on to save my life.
So I shan't press the point in any detail;
I grant you helped me, and I'm glad you did.
On the other hand, you got more than you gave.
The first thing is, you live in Greece, instead
Of somewhere barbarous; you have learned of justice,
To enjoy the rule of law – not the whim of despots.
Then, all the Greeks have heard of you, the wise one,
And you are famous; if you were still living
At the edge of the world, there'd be no talk of you.
For me, I wouldn't want a houseful of gold,
Or a finer singing voice than Orpheus –
Unless mankind could hear and point me out.

[I've said that much about the Labours of Jason
Only because you put the subject forward.]
You also reproach me for my royal marriage:
I'm going to show you that was well thought out,
Entirely prudent, not a mindless impulse:
I was acting as the greatest possible friend
For you, and for my children – just keep calm.

When I moved on from Iolcos and came here,
Dragging misfortune inescapably
Behind me, what better treasure-trove could I have found
Than marriage with the daughter of a king – I, an exile?
Now don't torment yourself: don't think I'm weary
Of your bed; or that I'm smitten with desire
For a fresh wife – or have some strange ambition

To rival others who have many children –
Those that I have suffice – I've no complaint – of them
or you.

I acted solely to ensure that we live well
And never go without, because I know
People will shun a man who's lost his wealth.
Also, I hoped to bring my children up
In a manner worthy of my own descent;
I thought I'd breed some brothers for our sons,
Make them all equal, bring our lines together.
That way our happiness and security lies.
You don't need children – you have had enough –
But I could make my sons to come be useful
To those that I have now – is that a bad ambition?

You would approve – except that the marriage irks you.
Isn't that like a woman? You believe
While bed is right that everything is right,
But if you're left alone between the sheets
You treat your nearest, dearest and best friend
As your worst enemy. We should make our children
Some other way – and have no breed of women.
Then we would live as happy as the gods.

CHORUS: Jason, your speech is jewelled. All the same
We disagree with you, perhaps unwisely:
We think deserting her can not be right.

MEDEA: I seem to differ from so many people.
To me, a person who does wrong and then defends it
So plausibly, deserves the heaviest punishment.
He trusts his clever tongue to decorate
His crimes with pretty words, which makes him bold
Enough for anything – but he's not that clever.
That goes for you: don't dazzle me with words
And surface logic. One simple point will throw
Your argument and pin you to the ground.
If you'd been honest, you'd have talked it over:

Persuaded me first, and married her after –
Not kept it secret from those who loved you best.

JASON: And fine support you'd have given me if I'd told you
About this possible marriage, when even now
You hug your anger and will not give it up.

MEDEA: That wasn't what prevented you from speaking.
Wasn't it really the thought of being married
To a barbarian, and getting old –
And your great reputation in decline?

JASON: Try understanding: it was not for lust
I climbed into my present royal bed.
I did it, as I said before, to keep
You safe – and for my children: to breed them brothers
Who would be kings, to comfort us and keep us.

MEDEA: What painful comfort! I pray I never find it,
Or prosper in a way that blights the heart!

JASON: Oh, pray for something wiser: pray instead,
"Help me: not to find pain in what is pleasant,
And not to feel unlucky, when I'm not."

MEDEA: What arrogance, when you've got a safe retreat
And I'm alone and going into exile.

JASON: You chose this course yourself; blame no one else.

MEDEA: I chose it! How? Did I take a wife and leave you?

JASON: You cursed the king, and cursed his royal house.

MEDEA: Yes, and I'll be a curse to your house too.

JASON: I'll not go on with this. There is no point.
But if you want some help from my estate
Towards your exile and the children's needs,
Say so: I'm ready to be generous,
And give you letters for my friends abroad
Who'll treat you well. Don't be so passionate, woman.
Listen to me, to refuse such help is mad.

MEDEA: I'll make no use of any of your friends,
　　　　Nor will I take your bounty; give me nothing.
　　　　[There is no profit in a bad man's gifts.]

JASON: Well then, I ask the gods to be my witness
　　　　I only wish to serve you and the children
　　　　In every way; but you do not like kindness;
　　　　You wilfully push the help of friends away.
　　　　Because of this you are going to suffer more.

MEDEA: Go, go: I see you've been so long away
　　　　From her, you're itching with desire
　　　　For your new-broken girl. Get on with being married,
　　　　While you still can. Because I prophecy:
　　　　Your marriage will be one of horror and regret.

　　　Exit JASON.

CHORUS: Eros at times comes over us too strong,
　　　　　　Which wrecks our reputation
　　　　And leads us into doing wrong.
　　　But if she comes in moderation,
　　　　　　No goddess can delight you
　　　　　　As much as Aphrodite.
　　　　　　I beg you, heavenly mistress,
　　　Don't draw your golden bow at me, to fire
　　　Those arrows tipped with ointments of desire,
　　　　　　Which never miss.

O Chastity, the gods' best gift, embrace me;
　　　　　　Bring Self-control, instead
　　　　Of letting Aphrodite chase me
　　　Half-mad to someone else's bed,
　　　　　　Loading my days and nights
　　　　　　With quarrels, moods and fights.
　　　　　　I hope that she respects
　　　The quiet of all peaceful marriage beds
　　　And judges right whose bodies and whose heads
　　　　　　To stir with sex.

Dear country and dear home,
O may I never lose my city
And have to roam
Unhelped through life's impenetrable maze,
A pain we all can pity.
I'd rather die than live such days:
There is no fate so bad as being banned
For ever
From home, to see the world but never
Your native land.

I've seen, I did not learn
This tale from others, that no city
Will shelter you;
No guest of yours remembers you and treats
Your sufferings now with pity.
I curse the man who coldly meets
A fallen friend like that. Unlock your heart
I say,
Give him the freedom of your house,
Give him the key.

Enter AEGEUS.

AEGEUS: Medea!
I wish you happiness – how can anyone
Better begin, when talking to his friend?

MEDEA: Aegeus! How do you come to be here in Corinth?

AEGEUS: I've been at Apollo's ancient oracle.

MEDEA: Delphi, the middle of the world! Why there?

AEGEUS: To ask for the blessing of a child of my own seed.

MEDEA: You've lived till now and still you have no children?

AEGEUS: I have no heir; some god or fate prevents it.

MEDEA: And what words of advice did the oracle give?

AEGEUS: Wise words, but too subtle for a man to grasp.

MEDEA: Am I allowed to hear them?

AEGEUS: Certainly: it requires a clever mind.

MEDEA: Then tell me. What did it say?

AEGEUS: I was told "not to unstop the wineskin's neck"...

MEDEA: Till when? Till you do what? Till you go where?

AEGEUS: Until I returned "to my native land".

MEDEA: All gods be with you. May you get what you desire.

AEGEUS: What's wrong? Why do you look so pale and
strained?

MEDEA: Aegeus, my husband is the worst man living.

AEGEUS: But why? What has he done?

MEDEA: He's taken another wife to run his house.

AEGEUS: What? Jason dares do such a shameful thing!

MEDEA: He does. And I, once loved, am now despised.

AEGEUS: Is he in love? Or, out of love with you?

MEDEA: It's love. It's passion. He's betrayed his family.

AEGEUS: Forget him – if he's as bad as you say he is.

MEDEA: He is in love with royalty and power.

AEGEUS: Tell me everything. Who is the father?

MEDEA: Creon, who is the king of Corinth here.

AEGEUS: I see. Now I understand the reason for your despair.

MEDEA: This is the end of everything. I'm to be banished.
Creon means to drive me out of Corinth.

AEGEUS: And Jason lets him? That is shameful.

MEDEA: He does protest, he says – but happily
Endures the prospect of my banishment.
Aegeus, I beg you,
Take pity on me, pity my misfortune.
Don't stand by as they drive me out.
Receive me in your country, in your home.
And in return the gods will give you
The children you desire. You'll end a happy man.
You do not know how fate has favoured you
In bringing us together: for I have
Such remedies. I can cure your childless state.

AEGEUS: There are many reasons, lady, why I would
Dearly like to help you: first, to please the gods,
Then for your promise of children –
For there I am completely powerless.
But I make this condition: you reach my country
And I shall do my best as your protector
To guard your rights. But that is all I promise.
I am unable to help your flight from Corinth;
If you arrive in Athens at my house
You shall be safe: I'll give you up to no one.
But you must travel out of here yourself:
I cannot abuse the kindness of my host.

MEDEA: So be it. But you must confirm your promise
With an oath. Then I will rest content.

AEGEUS: Why, don't you trust me? What is troubling you?

MEDEA: I trust you; but the house of Pelias
Is my enemy, and Creon too.
If you are bound by oaths, you cannot yield me
To any enemies.
[With just your word, not sworn by any gods,
You might become their friend and yield perhaps
To their diplomacy.] My state is weak,
They have the power of a royal house.

AEGEUS: Medea, you are looking far ahead!
　　　　But I'll not refuse to do as you think best.
　　　　In fact, the oath will be security for me –
　　　　A good excuse to give your enemies.
　　　　It makes your standing firmer too. Well then,
　　　　Begin: tell me the gods that I must swear by.

MEDEA: Swear by this dust of Earth, by Helios the Sun,
　　　　My father's father; then, by all the gods together.

[AEGEUS: What must I swear to do, or not do? Tell me.

MEDEA: That you will never banish me yourself,
　　　　Nor will you, if my enemies want to take me,
　　　　Release me to them willingly, while you live.]

AEGEUS: I swear by Earth, by the clear lamp of Helios,
　　　　By all the gods, I shall abide by what you say.

MEDEA: I am content. But if you don't abide
　　　　By this strong oath, what penalty should you suffer?

AEGEUS: The fate of those who don't respect the gods.

MEDEA: Be happy in your journey. All's well now.
　　　　I shall come to your city very soon –
　　　　When I have finished what I've got to do
　　　　[And hit the targets that I've set myself].

Exit AEGEUS as the CHORUS give the travel-blessing.
NURSE appears at door of Palace.

CHORUS: May Hermes bring you safe to Athens,
　　　　　You noble man.
　　　　And may you get the blessing you desire,
　　　　　A noble son.

MEDEA: O Zeus! O Justice of Zeus! O Helios!

　　　　Now we are winning; we shall stand in triumph
　　　　Over my enemies. We have begun to move.

Just when we seemed caught helpless in the storm,
This man appears, and offers me safe harbour.
Now I shall tell you what I'm going to do.

I'll send a servant who will ask for Jason
To come and see me; and when Jason comes,
I'll lull him with soft words and calmly say,
"Yes, I agree with you, it's quite the best decision
To leave us, to make a royal marriage:
It's in all our interests, a clever move."
Then I shall ask him if our sons can stay –
I'll use them as messengers of death to Creon's child.
I'll send them to her with presents in their hands,
A long light veil and a wreath of beaten gold,
But I shall smear such ointments on each one
That when she takes these ornaments and puts them
Against her skin, she will die horribly –
And everyone who touches her will die.

All that is easy, but I weep
To think of what comes next, what must be done,
And done by me: I'm going to kill
My children. Nobody shall take them from me.
Then, with the house of Jason quite destroyed,
I shall escape from Corinth, and escape
The penalty of killing my dear sons,
The most unholy crime we can commit.
I cannot, will not tolerate the scorn
Of those I hate. So let it all come down.
What life have I to lose?
What a mistake I made, that day I left
My father's house, believing in the words
Of a Greek. But he shall pay the price:
He'll never see the sons he got on me
Alive again, nor will he father one
On his new-harnessed bride, because she's doomed.
Let no one think Medea mild and quiet
And meek: I am of another mould,

Gentle to friends, implacable to foes.
That is the way to be respected here.

CHORUS: You have made us share your plans. You have
made us promise
To help you, but we have to take the side
Of human law. We therefore say: don't do this.

MEDEA: No other way. Your words can be forgiven,
Because you have not suffered; but I have.

CHORUS: But woman, how can you bear to kill your children?

MEDEA: It is the way to hurt my husband most.

CHORUS: And make yourself the most miserable of women.

MEDEA: Let be – all words are vain from now till then.

To NURSE.

Come on then; go; you, go and fetch me Jason:
It's always you when I need someone I can trust.
You will say nothing of what I plan to do,
If you care for your mistress, if you are a woman.

Exit NURSE.

CHORUS: The Athenians have been flourishing
And happy ever since
The gods first sowed them in that holy land –
It is a Holy Land, unravaged, where they feed
On Wisdom, the ambrosia of thought –
Filing so elegantly through that brilliant air
Where once, the Athenians say,
The virgin Muses came
And bore their fair-haired child, Harmonia.

That lovely stream of Cephisus
Is where the Queen of Love
Draws her moist breath and breathes it out across
Their country, puffs of moderate breeze with her sweet
scent.

There all year round she decorates her hair
With a fresh crown of woven flowers, perfumed roses –
   And she controls her child;
   For Eros there is good:
She makes him work for virtue and the arts.

So how will that city of holy rivers
That country hospitable to friends,
Take in the murderess of her sons,
Unclean among its citizens?
Imagine doing a child harm.
Imagine cutting and killing him.
We beg you every way we can:
   Do not kill your children.

Where in your heart will you find the daring,
How will you nerve the hand and breast
With the awful courage it must take
To maim the bodies you love best?
When you look down and raise your knife,
When they look up and beg for life,
The tears will stop you, you will not
   Stain your hands with children.

Enter JASON with NURSE.

JASON: I've come. I'm at your command. I know you hate me,
  But I could not refuse you: I shall listen.
  So, you want something new from me. What is it?

MEDEA: Jason, I'm asking you to be forgiving
  About the things I said. You should indulge
  My anger, after all our acts of friendship.
  I have begun to take myself to task:
  "Obstinate, silly woman, you must be mad:
  Why are you so opposed to good advice?"
  Why make myself an enemy of the king
  And of my husband, who is acting only
  In our best interest, marrying a princess

To give my children brothers? Will I never
Curb my temper? What's wrong with me? The gods
Provide so well for everything I need.
I've got children, haven't I? Have I forgotten
That we're in exile here and have no friends?
Thinking about it, I have seen how little
I plan ahead, blinded by futile anger.
So now I agree with everything you proposed.
You made a sound and practical alliance
On our behalf, while I was merely thoughtless:
I should have helped you plan the match, perhaps
As go-between. I could have stood beside
Your bed, with pleasure tending your new wife.
But we are what we are. I am a woman.
Not wicked perhaps, but frail. But it was wrong of you
To imitate my frailty and reply
With childish answers to my childishness.
But that's all past. I admit that I was wrong,
Before. I am wiser now. I ask your pardon.

Enter CHILDREN and TUTOR from the palace.

Oh, children, here; children, don't stay inside.
Welcome your father, come and talk to him,
Give up your hatred as your mother has.
We have made peace; our anger's soothed away.
So take his hand, his right hand – O my dears!

JASON is startled. She covers up.

I thought of the pain the future hides from us.
O children! may you live long years like this
Holding out your arms ... What a fool I am
To weep so easily, to be so frightened.
Here I am, ending the quarrel with your father
At last, and I blur the tender sight with tears.

CHORUS: Pale tears have started from my eyes too.
　　O may this evil go no further!

JASON: This is much better, woman; this is good –
    But I don't blame you for your other moods.
    It's natural for a woman to be angry
    With her husband embarking on a second marriage.
    But now your mind has moved to better thoughts:
    You've seen the winning strategy, in the end,
    Which proves you can control yourself and think.
    And you, my sons, your father's spent much thought
    On you – I've made arrangements. You'll be safe,
    With the gods' help. One day you will come back
    And be the foremost here in Corinth, with your brothers.
    What you must do is grow; leave all the rest
    To your father – and the friendly gods.
    I look to see you reaching, strong and well,
    To the full mark of manhood, taller than my enemies!

    But what are these fresh tears? Why are you crying
    Instead of being glad at what I say?

MEDEA: It's nothing. I was thinking of the children.

JASON: Take heart then: I'm making good provision for them.

MEDEA: I'll try – it's not that I distrust your words.
    A woman's naturally soft and given to tears.

JASON: (*Persists.*)
    You seem so mournful over them. Why's that?

MEDEA: I bore them, Jason. When you talked of their great
                                   future,
    Sadness came over me; life is so uncertain.

    But now, you came so we could talk. I've said
    Some of it, and I'll try to say the rest.
    The king sees fit to send me out of Corinth,
    And I agree – I understand – it's best
    If I live somewhere else, not in your way
    Or in the king's – because he thinks I hate him.

So I'll be exiled – I am going soon –
But the children – you should bring them up yourself:
Ask Creon not to banish them as well.

JASON: I don't know I'd persuade him; one should try...

MEDEA: In that case, get your wife to ask her father
This favour: not to banish them from Corinth.

JASON: Certainly; her, I think I can persuade.

MEDEA: If she's a woman like all other women...

[This time I'll take a hand and do my share:]
I'll send her presents, the most beautiful things,
By far, that any person living has –
Our sons shall carry them.

                        Go, children,
Bring the treasures to us right away.

The CHILDREN go into the palace.

She shall have not one happiness, but many,
Not only catching a hero for a husband,
But also the adornments that the Sun,
My father's father, gave to his descendants.

JASON: Why do you give away your greatest treasures?
Do you think the royal house is short of clothes?
Or needs more gold? Don't give your rich inheritance away.
Surely, if I'm worth anything to my bride,
She'll pay more heed to me than to these gifts.

MEDEA: Don't be so sure. They tell us gifts can sway
Even the gods, and when it comes to mortals,
Bright gold is stronger than ten thousand words.
[Fate's on her side, and makes her fortune grow,
She's young and she's in power.
But] to save my sons from exile
I'd barter with my life, never mind gold.

The CHILDREN return with partly-wrapped presents.

Take good care of these wedding presents, children,
Carry them properly
To the princess, the lucky bride: she'll have
Presents from me that nobody could fault.

And listen now: when you reach the palace,
Find your father's new wife, my mistress now,
And ask her, beg her: not to have you banished;
Give her these fine things – this is most important –
Give them into her hands alone.
Go quickly now. May all go well.
And bring your mother the news she longs to hear.

JASON leaves with the CHILDREN and TUTOR.

CHORUS: Now there's no hope, not any more, for the
children's lives.
They are walking at this moment towards death.
The young wife will be taking in the golden bands,
She will be thanking them for her destruction,
As on her yellow hair she sets
Her finery for the underworld, with her own hands.

Persuaded by their beauty, their immortal glow,
She will put on the veil, the golden crown,
Dressing the bride herself for those who wait below.
She will be tripping in the snare and falling
Into the trap of destiny
And wretched death: it's closing, and she won't get free.

You, wicked bridegroom, you shall suffer too:
Marrying into power, you have brought,
Not knowing what you do,
Disaster to your children, to your wife
A horrible end.
How you have wandered from the hero's life!

And I must weep to see your painful doom,
Unhappy mother, who will kill
The children of your womb

Because a treacherous husband left his place
        Between your arms
And broke the law, to kiss a different face.

Re-enter TUTOR with CHILDREN. NURSE still on
through this scene.

TUTOR: Mistress, your sons have been released from exile.
    The royal bride was pleased to take the presents
    In her own hands.
    The children have been spared. They have a truce.
    What's the matter? They and you are lucky.

MEDEA: How cruel.

TUTOR: What have I said? I thought it was good news.

MEDEA: You told us what you told us: I don't blame you.

TUTOR: Then why are you staring at the ground? Why are
                                you weeping?

MEDEA: How can I help it? – when I think the gods
    And my own wicked thoughts have worked to make
                          this happen.

TUTOR: Take heart; some day the boys will come to Athens
    And bring you back from exile, down to Corinth.

MEDEA: Ah, before that, I shall bring others down.

TUTOR: You're not the only woman to be separated
    From her children: we must learn to bear things lightly.

MEDEA: I'll try to do so. But go in. Get the children
    Whatever they need – like any other day.

The TUTOR goes in. The CHILDREN stay.

Oh children, children – so you have a city:
You'll have a home, to go and stay in always –
Away from your mother, leaving me to grieve.
For I am going somewhere else, to exile,

Before I get the joy of you and see
Your happiness, your weddings and your wives,
Before I decorate your marriage beds
Or hold the wedding torches over you.

What misery I have chosen for myself!
I suckled you, my children, but for nothing –
My labour went for nothing, all the scratches
Of fortune's claws, and crushing pangs of birth.
Such hope, I had such hopes of you:
That you would care for me when I was old;
When I died, your hands would wrap me for the grave –
The final wish of man. Those dreams were sweet
But they have come to nothing: bereft of you,
I shall drag out a life of pain and grief,
While you will never see your mother again
With those dear eyes, but change into another life.
My children, why are you staring at me so?
Why do you smile at me, that last of all your smiles?
What am I going to do? My heart gives way,
It betrays me, when I see their shining faces,
My babies. I cannot do it. Forget all plans
I made before. I'll take my boys with me.
How can I harm them just to hurt their father,
When all his pain would be as nothing to mine?
I will not do it. [No. Goodbye, my plans.]

What's happening to me? Do I really want
To leave my enemies mocking me – and unpunished?
I must be brave, and do it. Coward woman,
To let soft arguments invade my heart...
Go, children; in; go in.

*The CHILDREN start to go, but hesitate. She forgets them
and speaks the next line to the CHORUS:*

                                    And anyone
Who has no right to attend the sacrifices
Of this household, keep away:

My hand's not going to weaken.
No! No!
No, raging heart, don't drive yourself to this.
Not this! Not the children's lives: let them alone.
They'll live there with us – they will bring us joy.
No, by the vengeful spirits that live in Hades,
I shall not leave my children, I cannot leave them
To suffer the violence of my enemies.

It's all done now, in any case: there's no escape.
Surely the crown is on her head by now,
And in her golden veil the bride lies dying.
It's done.
          And now I take the road of dreadful misery,
And set my children on a worse road yet
[I have to speak to them].

To the CHILDREN.

Oh, flesh of my flesh! Give me your hands,
And let your mother kiss your hands,
Your arms, your lips. O clear and noble face
And form of children! Now may you both be happy
But somewhere else – for here your father takes
All happiness to himself. O those sweet kisses,
And soft, soft skin – the gentle smell of childhood!
Go now, go, go.

The CHILDREN now enter the palace.

                      I can not look at them
One moment longer: this evil is overwhelming.
I know what I intend to do is wrong,
But the rage of my heart is stronger than my reason –
That is the cause of all man's foulest crimes.

She sits and waits, looking towards Corinth.

CHORUS: [I have been thinking – for women too
       Have a Muse that visits our thoughtless days –

I have been asking, as men might ask,]
What is this human desire for children?
Does it make sense? Perhaps it is better
To stay virgin, never to know
If sons and daughters bring in the end
A taste of sweetness or bitter pain.

Look at the parents, look at their eyes,
The radiant lines of love and worry.
"Is there enough for us all to eat?
Are they warm and well? Will they lead good lives
Or grow up bad?" These are the thoughts
That carve the faces of those who engender
The new generation. For behind the thoughts
Is a terrible fear: We know that Fate
May suddenly come with casual hand
And pick the children to die before us.

So what is the answer? Why do we persist
In the longing for children? Can't we see
They are only a target more for the marksmen
Who watch our lives from above?

MEDEA: At last. At last – there's one of Jason's servants.
I've waited here so long for news from the palace.
He comes towards us. He fights for breath –
Perhaps that shows the kind of news he brings.

Enter MESSENGER.

MESSENGER: Medea, you've done a terrible thing. Beyond
All laws of man. You must get away – escape
By land, or sea, anything: go, at once.

MEDEA: What's so terrible that I must fly my home?

MESSENGER: She's dead, our newly married princess; Creon
Her father, also; dying from your poisons.

MEDEA: Your message is beautiful; you shall count forever
Among my benefactors and my friends.

MESSENGER: What are you saying? Woman, are you mad –
Exulting at the pain you have inflicted
Upon our royal house? You do not flinch
To hear the terrible report of it?

MEDEA: I have an answer; I could counter that.
But tell your story slowly. Take the time.
My friend, how did they die? It will delight
Me twice as much if they died horribly.

MESSENGER: When your two little boys, beside their father,
Came hand in hand into the bridal house,
We were so happy, we, the slaves, who shared
With you your pain. The rumour spread from one
To another: you and your husband had healed your quarrel.
One kissed the hands, and one the small fair heads
Of your children. Drawn by happiness, I followed
Behind them to the princess's part of the house.
The mistress – whom we honour now, as once
We honoured you – had only eyes for Jason.
But when she saw your boys in the door together,
She dropped her gaze and coldly turned
Her pale young cheek away, as in disgust
That they were in her room. Your husband tried
To smooth away her anger and disdain
By saying, "Don't be cross with them – they're children;
Stop feeling angry, turn your head this way,
Think of your husband's family as your own,
Accept their gifts – and ask your father to release
My children from their exile, for my sake."

She saw the gifts they bore – could not resist,
Agreed to all her new-made husband wanted.
Your children and their father had scarcely left
The room before she'd picked the lace-veil up,
And wrapped it round herself, and on her brow
Settled the golden crown. She rearranged
Her hair with a bright mirror in one hand,
And smiled at the lifeless image of herself.

Then suddenly this pleasant scene turned to horror

Then she stood up, delighted with her presents.
She paced around so elegantly, turning
To see the folds of finery at her ankles.
Then suddenly this pleasant scene turned to horror:
Her colour changed, she paled, she staggered back
Into her chair, trembling in every limb.
One of her older women, thinking maybe
Some god of frenzy was attacking her,
Started to intone a prayer, but saw her mouth
Ran with bright scum, her eyes were turning back
Into her skull, no blood was in her skin.
The chant of her prayer became a shriek.
The servants of the house ran off
To fetch the father, to fetch the husband,
To tell them the disaster. The whole palace
Resounded to the thud of running feet.

Long, long moments she lay, with close-shut eyes,
In a speechless trance,
Then woke, poor girl, and gave a terrible cry.
A second torment opened its attack:
The golden garland clinging to her hair
Melted in a torrent of omnivorous flame,
And the delicate gown, your children's gift to her,
Began devouring the poor girl's delicate flesh.
She rose out of her chair and ran, on fire
Shaking her hair, her head, this way and that
Trying to throw the crown off; but the gold
Gripped strong and firm, and the flame blazed up
Still more, increasing when she shook her hair.
She fell to the floor, exhausted by the pain,
Past recognition now, even to her father –
The setting of her eyes, the lovely face
No longer showed, but blood, entwined with flame
Fell from the crown of her head in gouts and spurts,
And from her bones dripped flesh like pinetree tears,
The invisible teeth of poison pulping it,
A sight so horrible we were all afraid
To touch the corpse: the terror had taught us caution.

But her poor father, not knowing how she'd died,
Coming in suddenly, fell upon the body
Folding his arms about the corpse
And crying aloud, "My child, my child,
What god has destroyed you in this abominable way?
Who robs an old man close to the grave of an only child?
May I die – let me die beside my daughter."
His tears and laments stilled at last,
He tried to lift his aged body up,
But the delicate gown clung fast like tangling ivy
On a laurel branch: a dreadful wrestling match.
He struggled to his knees, the sparkling dress
Holding him down, and as he used his strength
He tore the age-worn flesh from off his bones.
Fainting at last, no longer able to resist,
He gave to his unhappy soul release.
So they lie dead, the daughter and the father,
Together – a relief that gave us tears.

Directly to MEDEA.

What happens to you I do not wish to think of –
You will know some way to escape their vengeance.
But I must think, as I have thought before,
That human life is nothing but a shadow,
Nor would I hesitate to say that clever men,
Or those reputed clever, who play with words,
Are wrong – they should be called the greatest fools:
No mortal man is happy – safe from god.
Oh, if wealth pours down, one human might become
More prosperous than another – but happy, no.

CHORUS: The gods came down today and heaped on Jason
    A terrible punishment, but it was deserved.

Exit MESSENGER towards Corinth.

MEDEA: Well then, it is decided: I must do it
    And quickly: kill the children, leave the country;

No time, not a moment's delay lest I surrender
My sons for some unkinder hand to kill.
[They'll have to die in any case: and therefore]
I'll kill them – I'm the one who gave them life.
Come heart, fasten your armour. Why delay
The awful but inevitable crime?
Come wretched hand, my hand, pick up the sword,
And creep towards the starting-line of pain.
No cowardice! No memories of the children
Being lovely, being born – for this short day
Forget your boys – weep for them afterwards:
For though you're going to kill them, they were loved –
While I was born unlucky and a woman.

Exit NURSE and MEDEA.

CHORUS: O Earth, O Helios shining everywhere
          Look down your rays and see
This deadly woman now before she kills
And reddens her white hands with children's gore.
          It's her own blood she spills
But also yours: they are your golden seed.
          A fearful thing, to pour
          A god's blood on the ground,
A god's blood dripping from a human hand.
O light of heaven, prevent her, intercede
Against Medea, the Fury of this house,
Unhappy, murderous, driven to revenge.

Your work of having children goes to waste,
          Your labour and your love,
All wasted, all since you became a wife,
Since you came down the cruel passage, through
          The clashing rocks of life.
Poor wretch, why did this weight of anger fall
          So heavily on you?
          And why did murder find
A place among the answers in your mind?

The stain of family blood is hard to bear
For us on earth: when someone kills his kin,
The gods themselves come down to take revenge.

A CHILD screams offstage.

CHORUS: Do you hear the cries? Do you hear the children?
Unhappy woman, woman of misery.

BOYS: (*Offstage cries.*)
[What can I do to escape from mother's hands?
– I don't know, brother. We are going to die.]

CHORUS: Dare we go in? We ought, we ought.
To protect the children.

BOYS: (*Offstage cries.*)
[Protect us! Yes, we need your help. Come quick.
– We are nearly in the net: the sword will catch us.]

CHORUS: Wretched woman, you must be made
Of stone or iron, to cut your crop
Of children down, making your hand
The hand of Fate.
One woman only before our time
Has ever laid hands on her own children.

But that was Ino, who was driven mad
By jealous Hera. Medea is not mad.

When Ino killed her little boys,
She jumped into the sea. But Medea is not mad.

She wandered to the edge of a sea cliff
And fell and drowned. But Medea is not mad.

What further horror is left to happen?
O marriage, bed of women,

Bed of pain, how much harm
You have done to mortal man!

Enter JASON, in haste.

JASON: You, women –
    Is she – I cannot say the name; she's done
    Such terrible things – is she still here? – Medea?
    Has she hidden away? She'd have to cower
    Under the earth or else grow wings and rise
    To the deepest layer of heaven, to escape
    Being punished for the royal house of Corinth.
    Did she think to kill the rulers of the country,
    Then leave this house and get away scot-free?
    But it's my sons I'm anxious for, not her:
    The family she has harmed will see to her,
    But I have come to save my children's lives:
    I fear the royal clan may take revenge
    On me and mine for their mother's bloody deed.

CHORUS: Poor Jason! Poor man! You still don't seem to know
    How bad it is – how far your misery goes.

JASON: What deeper misery? Will she kill me too?

CHORUS: Your sons are dead, and by their mother's hand.

JASON: What, dead? Who, dead? Woman, you're killing me.

CHORUS: Your children are no longer living.

JASON: She killed them? Where? In the house? Where?

CHORUS: Open the doors: you'll see them, slaughtered.

JASON: Unbar the doors. Let me see.
    Let me see my murdered sons.
    Let me see them dead, and let me take revenge.

    *As JASON pounds on the doors, MEDEA appears high up
    in the house. Near her lie the CHILDREN's corpses, ready
    to be displayed.*

MEDEA: What are you doing [breaking down the doors]?
    Searching for corpses and the woman who made them?
    Stay there. If you have need of me, then say so:

Open the doors: you'll see them, slaughtered.

Say what you like; you can never touch me, now.
[Not in this chariot which my father's father,
The Sun, has given me for my protection.]

JASON: You hateful woman, abominable thing,
Loathed by the gods and me and all mankind!,
You could pick up a sword and hack the bodies
Of children you had borne, to leave me childless.
You have done this and dare to face the Sun
And Earth! Oh harsh and sacrilegious heart!
I curse you – now, in my right mind at last,
Not senseless as I was when from your home,
That barbarous place, I brought you back with me
To a civilised land, already evil then.
The avenging demon who was meant for you
The gods have turned on me – you killed your brother,
The boy who shared your childhood: foul with blood
You stepped aboard my lovely boat, the Argo.
So you began; and after lying as a wife
Beside me, after bearing sons to me,
From jealousy and lust you kill them too.
No woman born in Greece could bring herself
To such an act, and yet in preference to them
I chose to marry you, I chose the hand
Of the enemy who was going to destroy me,
A tiger, a savage, not a woman.
Ah, but a million insults could not bite
Into your heart, it is so brazen hard.
Go, monstrous spirit, stained with children's blood.
Out of my sight. Leave me to weep, and rail
Upon the god who minds my destiny:
That I shall never enjoy my new-found bride,
Never hold my sons again in my arms.
All, all; all is lost; I lost them all.

MEDEA: I could reply to everything you've said.
But Zeus, father of gods and men, has witnessed all
I did for you and all you did to me.

You were not fated to insult my bed
And live on pleasantly, laughing in my face,
Nor was your princess. Nor was the father Creon –
Who gave her to you – allowed to banish me
Without retaliation. Call me savage,
Call me a tigress, call me what you like.
But I have reached you. I have struck your heart.

JASON: And hurt yourself: you share the loss and pain.

MEDEA: The cry of your pain is music. It eases mine.

JASON: My sons, what an unnatural mother you were given!

MEDEA: Children,
      Your father was ill with love: you died of it.

JASON: It was not my hand that has brought them death.

MEDEA: No, just the insult of your other marriage.

JASON: You thought it right to kill them for a marriage!

MEDEA: You think that pain was little, to a woman?

JASON: To a sane one, yes. But you find pain in everything.

MEDEA: Look: they are dead. That thought stings even you.

JASON: They live, as Furies to curse your blood.

[MEDEA: The gods know who began this agony.

JASON: Because they see the horrors of your mind.]

MEDEA: Hate on. How I detest your snarling voice.

JASON: And I loathe yours; parting from that is easy.

MEDEA: Well, what is left? I want it over too.

JASON: To bury and mourn them – let me have the bodies.

MEDEA: No. I shall bury them. These hands shall do it
      [When I have carried them to Hera's temple
      Where they'll be safe from insults of their enemies,

Who might dig up their graves; and in this land
Where Sisyphus was king, we'll institute
A holy festival and sacrifice
For ever, to expiate their sinful murder].
Then I shall go to the city of Athena,
To Aegeus' house, and live in peace with him.
But you shall have no hero's death, no glory:
You shall be crushed by a rotting timber of your Argo –
A bitter end to your marriage to Medea.

JASON: Then I call down the Fury of vengeance
For little children: Swoop and destroy her.

MEDEA: What kind of god do you think will listen
To a breaker of oaths, a deceiver of strangers?

JASON: Unclean, abhorrent, killer of children.

MEDEA: Go home. You can bury your wife.

JASON: I am going, bereft of my two sons.

MEDEA: These tears are nothing. Wait till you're old.

JASON: Oh my children, dear sons.

[MEDEA: To their mother, not you.

JASON: So dear that you killed them?

MEDEA: To give you pain.]

JASON: I long to kiss the gentle lips
Of my poor children.

[MEDEA: Now you talk to them, now you cling to them –
Then you rejected them.]

JASON: By the gods, allow me
To hold my sons' poor bodies one last time.

MEDEA: Nevermore. Your words are thrown away,
Mouthfuls of rubbish.

JASON: Zeus, do you hear? She refuses me that!
    Even that! You see what she's done to me!
    Look at this beast, fouled with blood.
    It is the blood of her own young.
    Nothing is left me, nothing to do
    But stand and cry like a woman to heaven.
    You killed my sons and now you deny me
    My right to touch them, to cradle, to bury them.
    Oh gods, I wish
    I had never bred these sons.
    Oh gods, I wish I had never lain
    In their mother's murderous arms.

    Pause.

CHORUS: And that is how it happened here.

    THE END

APPENDIX I

Ancient Greek plays have no stage directions. The earliest texts have no punctuation, no breaks between words and no indication of who is speaking, though they do sometimes indicate changes of speaker. It follows that all stage action, all props, all attribution of lines are the invention of later editors or translators, deriving entrances, exits and business from the actual words of the text.

The lack of stage-direction may be interpreted as conferring a certain freedom. In Jonathan Kent's production, at the Almeida, for instance, the Chorus were on stage at the start, instead of appearing when they first speak; also the set represented a courtyard inside the palace, instead of the outside, as originally.

The full text of certain passages may be thought preferable to the cut versions printed in the foregoing version:

1.

The *stichomythia* following Aegeus' entrance:

Enter AEGEUS, king of Athens, middle-aged. The audience knows he is going to be the father of THESEUS, the big Athenian hero; also that he is going to be MEDEA's next husband.

AEGEUS: Be happy, Medea – how can anyone
Better begin, when talking to his friends?

MEDEA: And you be happy, son of wise Pandion,
Aegeus! How do you come to pass through Corinth?

AEGEUS: I've been at Phoebus' ancient oracle.

MEDEA: Delphi, the middle of the world! Why there?

AEGEUS: I wanted help with sowing seed – for children.

MEDEA: By the gods, you've lived till now and had no child?

AEGEUS: Yes, I've no heir; some god or fate prevents it.

MEDEA: Have you a wife? Or have you not tried marriage?

AEGEUS: I have a marriage bed, with someone in it.

MEDEA: Well, what did Phoebus say about having children?

AEGEUS: Wise words – too clever for a man to grasp.

MEDEA: Would it be right for me to hear this oracle?

AEGEUS: Certainly: it demands a clever mind.

MEDEA: Then tell me the response – if that's allowed.

AEGEUS: I must not open the front end of my wineskin...

MEDEA: Till when? till you do what? till you go where?

AEGEUS: Till I get back "to the paternal fire".

MEDEA: But why have you sailed this way home, by Corinth?

AEGEUS: There's a man called Pittheus, who is king of
Troezen...

MEDEA: Son of Pelops. They say he's most religious.

AEGEUS: I want to put this oracle to him.

MEDEA: Indeed the man is clever, and experienced.

AEGEUS: Also, of all my allies, my best friend.

MEDEA: Good luck, then; may you get what you desire.

AEGEUS: Is something wrong? Your face is pale and wasted.

The Greek suggests he touches her face.

MEDEA: Aegeus, my husband is the worst man living.

AEGEUS: How? Tell me plainly why you're so unhappy.

MEDEA: Jason has wronged me. I'd given him no cause.

AEGEUS: What has he done then? Make it clearer to me.

MEDEA: He's got another wife to run his house.

AEGEUS: No! Did he dare do such a shameful thing!

MEDEA: He did. And we, once loved, are now disowned.

AEGEUS: Is he in love? Or, out of love with you?

MEDEA: It's love. It's passion. He betrayed his family.

AEGEUS: Forget him – if he's bad, as you've been saying.

MEDEA: The person that he wanted so is royal.

AEGEUS: Who is her father? Tell me all the rest.

MEDEA: Creon, who is the king of Corinth here.

AEGEUS: No wonder you're distressed. I hardly blame you.

MEDEA: Distressed? We're ruined! I'm being banished, too.

AEGEUS: Who's ordered that? Again, more dreadful news.

MEDEA: It's Creon who's expelling me from Corinth.

AEGEUS: And Jason lets him? That is wrong as well.

MEDEA: He does protest, he says – (etc.)

2.

The Chorus' rather long (but important) philosophical speech about the human desire for children:

CHORUS: A few times now
    I have come out with difficult words
    And ideas perhaps a little aggressive
    For my soft sex to chase the tracks of.
    But you see, we too have a Muse that visits
    And talks to us about clever things;
    Not to all of us – you might think few
    Among so many – but there are some
      Who meet this Muse of Thought.

What I say then is that in mortal life
Those who stay virgin, those who never
Engender children get nearer to happiness
Than any parent.
Those who are childless never find out
By their own experience if sons and daughters
Bring sweetness or pain: not having any
    They are saved much distress.
But those whose house has a sweet bed
Of growing children – I see them worn,
Worn out with worry right through their lives:
First about how to tend them well
And how to leave them something to live on,
And even then it remains unclear
Whether the objects of all their effort
Are good or bad.
But I shall tell you what the worst is
Of all bad things that happen to humans:
Suppose they have found enough to live on,
Suppose their bodies arrive at manhood,
And they are virtuous; still if their fate
Turns out that way, Death sweeps off
To Hades, taking your children's bodies.
So I say, what profit is there for mortals
In striving for children when we see the gods
Throwing on top of our other burdens
    This cruellest pain of all?

3.

The last lines of the play, the Chorus's final comment, lines
which also end some other Euripides plays, and are generally
regarded by scholars as spurious. In the Almeida production
these lines, but for the last, were cut:

CHORUS: Zeus on Olympus governs the world.
    The gods accomplish the unexpected.

What we foresee does not come true.
But the gods find a way to allow the unthinkable.
    And so it happened here.

APPENDIX II

THE FIRST STASIMON OF *MEDEA:* THREE VERSIONS

This article was first published in AD FAMILIARES, the journal of Friends of Classics, Vol. III, to whom we express our gratitude.

In September 1991 I was asked by Jonathan Kent, joint Artistic Director of the Almeida Theatre, Islington, to translate Euripides' *Medea* for Diana Rigg. There seemed to be a lot of *Medeas* around, both in translation and in production, but I accepted.

It seemed obvious (but still a conscious choice is involved) that the ordinary dialogue should be turned into English blank verse, and I did all that first, wondering if Euripides also had written the play before composing the choruses. How to do the choruses was a problem that hung over me as I worked through the dialogue. One recurring thought was that when you see a Greek tragedy done in Greek the choruses do not stand out as difficult: on the contrary, they are possibly the best bit. Perhaps this is why the Raphael and McLeish version at Manchester kept the choruses in Greek and made a singing ballet of them.

But when you are translating a play surely you have to do it all. The words of the Chorus are not unconnected with the play. I thought about the history of Greek tragedy and decided to take the line that the plays were originally musical performances that had been gradually taken over by their introducers and explainers: the disk-jockeys had become the show, as it were; and that therefore, the choral odes should be treated as almost a separate show interwoven with the play, separate but relevant, unlike the musical interludes in e.g., the Goon Show. They should be fun and attractive in their own right (Oh good, here comes the Chorus). Also, the musician's attitude to the audience is certainly different from the actor's, so the tone of their offerings should be different. I decided to write their words either as songs or as poetry for performance, with strong rhymes and metre.

I was pleased with the way the choruses turned out: the horrible apparently half-baked vagueness of choral lyrics as I remembered them from school seemed to disappear when I was forced to make a sensible English poem out of them. The first was even on the edge of being funny – "don't kill yourself because your husband's left you" is begging to be turned into a satirical song; but one got a gradual increase in seriousness as the chorus was forced more and more into sympathy and co-operation.

My director liked the first ode, but asked me to make the second one (the first stasimon) a bit earthier. Instead of tinkering, I rewrote the ode, going much too far in the direction of earthiness – a ranging shot, attempting to bracket the target. (Artillery methods are rather Aristotelian: the extremes and the middle way.) The third attempt seemed to me just about right. However, of course, my director liked bits of each. But they are in different stanza forms... Translation is endless.

I hope that reading all three of these versions will shed some light on the relevance of this ode to the adjacent parts of Euripides' great play. I add also as literal a version as a poet can bear to print.

A LITERAL VERSION

1 Uphill the waters [the top meaning of the word is "sources" or "springs"] of holy rivers go,/

and justice [the rules of ethics] and everything [presumably the rules of nature, which is everything] are being turned backwards;/

on one hand in men [or husbands] are [found] wily thoughts [this probably means husbands are using the wiles that women have previously had to use; but it also may mean that everybody's a crook nowadays], and trustworthy oaths sworn by the gods/

are no longer firm./

5 But on the other hand the voices [the reports, the fame-songs] will be turning my life so that it has good reputation;/

honour [civic rights] is coming to the race of women;/

no longer will ill-speaking voice [report, fame] hold women [in its grasp]./

And the muses of old-born songs will cease/

to make hymns of my untrustworthiness./

10 [This was able to happen before] because into our understanding/

Phoebus Apollo, leader of melodies,/

did not give divine [language reminiscent of the Delphic gift of prophecy] song from the lyre; [I say that] because [if he had] I would have sung back in opposition an ode/

on the race of males. And the long [passage of] time has [in it the ability]/

many things on the one hand to say [about] the share-of-destiny of us [women] and of men [or husbands] also.//

But on the other hand you, on the one hand etc etc...

FIRST TAKE

Uphill in holy river beds,   1
     Upstream the waters flow:
The laws of nature and society
   Reverse the way their currents go.

Now men are full of wiles and smiles and tricks,
They swear by heaven, but no promise sticks –
      While everybody says   5
        That women's ways
Are now the better ways to fame.
Women shall get some honour and their rights.
Harsh gossip shall no longer hold us down with shame.

      Time honoured poems of the past
        Are going to be adjusted:
They can't keep singing that a woman is
    An animal that can't be trusted.
You see, Apollo, prince of melody,   10
Never gave us the gift of poetry:
      No lyre, no inspiration
        For the feminine nation.
    You can be sure that if he had,
I would have turned those songs against the males.
The course of time shows men as well as we were bad.

SECOND TAKE

Today the rivers are flowing uphill!   1
The laws of nature are working still,
   But inside out.
And someone's reversed the laws of society:
Dirty tricks flower in great variety,
And the gods are asking "What happened to piety?"
   They've lost their clout.
But women are rising; respect and honours   5
Are going to be showered down upon us,
We shall get the rights we've never had
And never be shut away again
   In the box that's labelled Bad.

The old songs about us will be adjusted:
They called us animals that can't be trusted,
   That sort of thing.

You see, the god of poetic creation,   10
Apollo, never gave his inspiration
To a feminine member of the nation:
   We could not sing.
But if I got my fingers on a lyre
I'd make those masculine bards perspire.
In the long time since the world began
There have been some stories about the woman,
   But as many about the man.

THIRD TAKE

The rivers, with their river-gods inside them,   1
   Flow up, to higher ground.
The laws of nature and the laws of man
      Have turned around:
Men do the wiles and smiles, the cheating, now,
   Men will not keep the vows they swore,
While women shall find history reversing   5
The low esteem in which they lived before.
A woman soon will have both rights and honour;
She won't have gossip holding her in check
   And pouring insults on her.

The music of those lovely ancient songs
   Would say, Don't trust a woman;
We were compared to every kind of beast
     And found less human.
The trouble was, Apollo, god of song,   10
   Never passed on his poetic fire
To one of us. He liked us dumb and dancing
And chose no woman poet to inspire.
Otherwise, what an ode I'd sing on men!
The ages can tell tales of us, but husbands
   Have been as bad again!